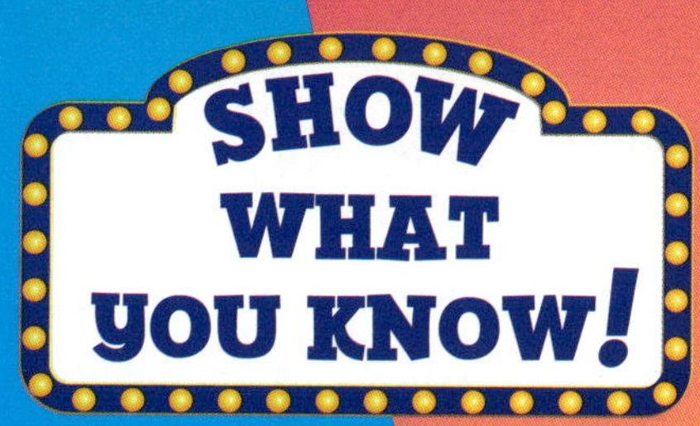

Finding the Right Words with Dictionaries

by Ann Truesdell

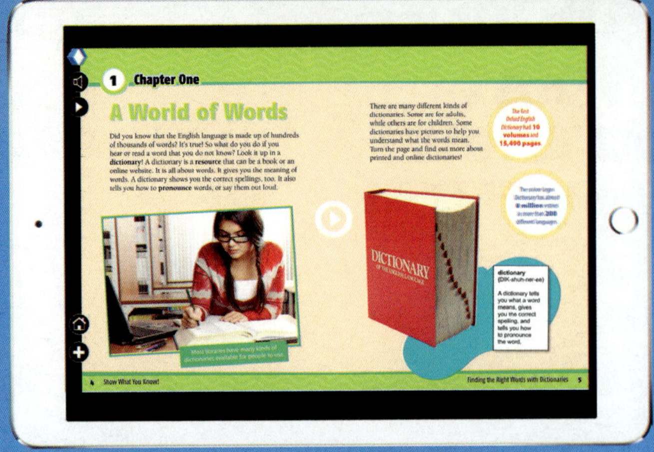

Lightbox is an all-inclusive digital solution for the teaching and learning of curriculum topics in an original, groundbreaking way. Lightbox is based on National Curriculum Standards.

STANDARD FEATURES OF LIGHTBOX

AUDIO High-quality narration using text-to-speech system

ACTIVITIES Printable PDFs that can be emailed and graded

SLIDESHOWS Pictorial overviews of key concepts

VIDEOS Embedded high-definition video clips

WEBLINKS Curated links to external, child-safe resources

TRANSPARENCIES Step-by-step layering of maps, diagrams, charts, and timelines

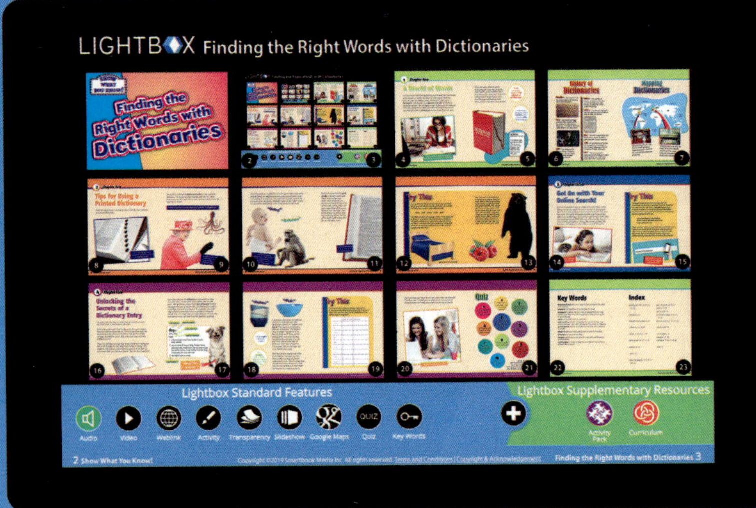

INTERACTIVE MAPS Interactive maps and aerial satellite imagery

QUIZZES Ten multiple choice questions that are automatically graded and emailed for teacher assessment

KEY WORDS Matching key concepts to their definitions

Finding the Right Words with Dictionaries

1 Chapter One

A World of Words

Did you know that the English language is made up of hundreds of thousands of words? It's true! So what do you do if you hear or read a word that you do not know? Look it up in a **dictionary**! A dictionary is a **resource** that can be a book or an online website. It is all about words. It gives you the meaning of words. A dictionary shows you the correct spellings, too. It also tells you how to **pronounce** words, or say them out loud.

Most libraries have many kinds of dictionaries available for people to use.

There are many different kinds of dictionaries. Some are for adults, while others are for children. Some dictionaries have pictures to help you understand what the words mean. Turn the page and find out more about printed and online dictionaries!

The first *Oxford English Dictionary* had **10 volumes** and **15,490 pages**.

The online Logos Dictionary has almost **8 million** entries in more than **200** different languages.

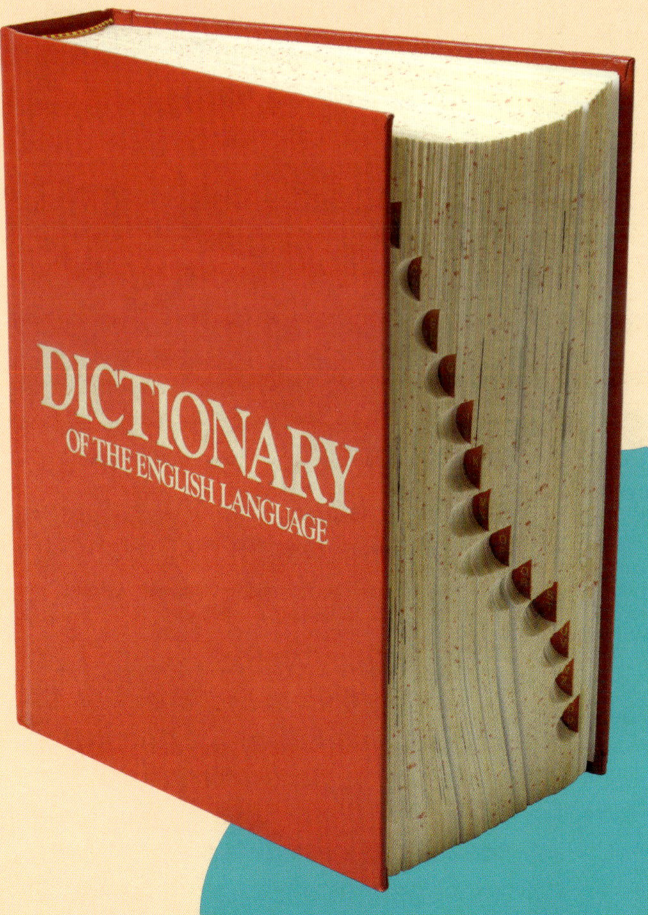

dictionary
(DIK-shuh-ner-ee)

A dictionary tells you what a word means, gives you the correct spelling, and tells you how to pronounce the word.

History of Dictionaries

200,000 BC Scientists believe the early ancestors of humans had simple languages.

8000 BC The people of Sumer, or what is now Iraq, carved symbols onto clay tablets, creating the oldest written language.

3000 BC The ancient Egyptians use the papyrus plant to make a type of paper for writing.

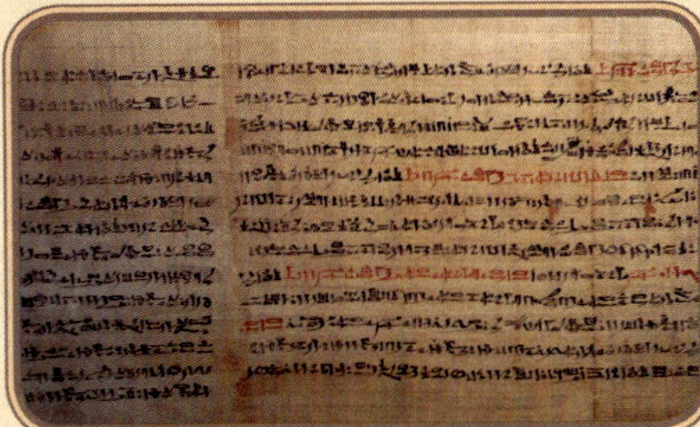

54 AD The Roman Emperor Claudius dies. During his life, he created the first bilingual dictionary. This type of dictionary gives words in two languages.

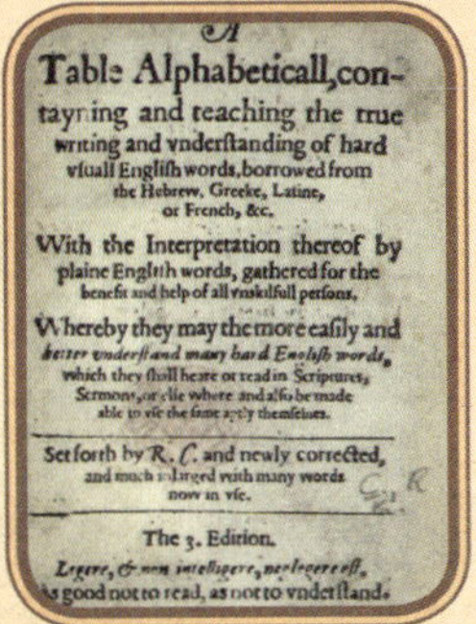

A
Table Alphabeticall, contayning and teaching the true writing and vnderſtanding of hard vſuall Engliſh words, borrowed from the Hebrew, Greeke, Latine, or French, &c.

With the Interpretation thereof by plaine Engliſh words, gathered for the benefit and help of all vnskilfull perſons.

Whereby they may the more eaſily and *better vnderſtand many hard Engliſh words*, which they ſhall heare or read in Scriptures, Sermons, or elſe where, and alſo be made able to vſe the ſame aptly themſelues.

Set forth by *R. C.* and newly corrected, and much enlarged with many words now in vſe.

The 3. Edition.

Legere, & non intelligere, neglegere eſt.
As good not to read, as not to vnderſtand.

1604 The first English-language dictionary is written by British schoolteacher Robert Cawdrey.

1806 Noah Webster publishes *A Compendious Dictionary of the English Language*, the first American English dictionary.

2010 The makers of the *Oxford English Dictionary* announce that the newest edition will be available only on the internet.

2017 The most popular dictionary in the world is China's *Xinhua Dictionary*, with more than 500 million copies sold.

Mapping Dictionaries

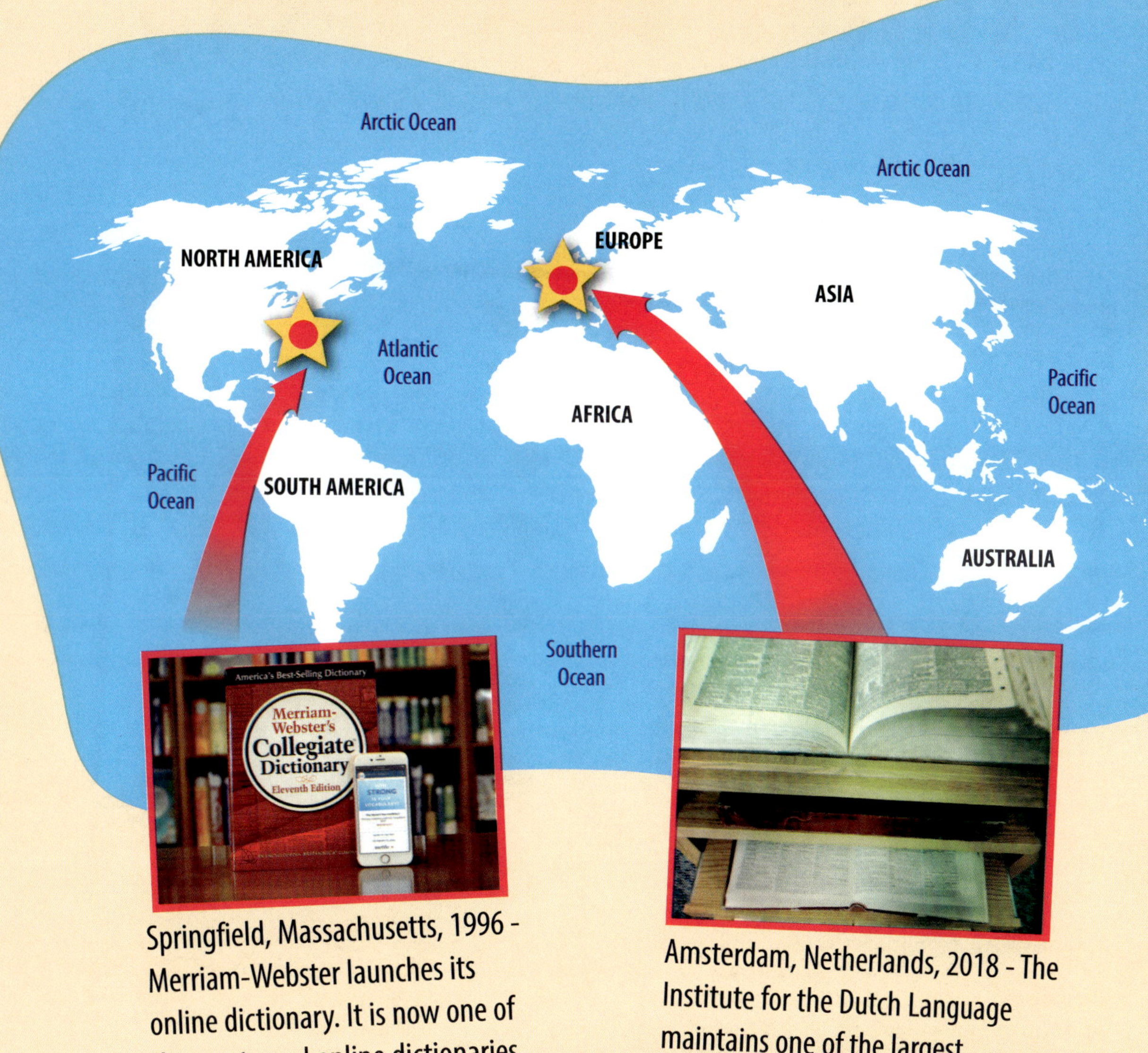

Springfield, Massachusetts, 1996 - Merriam-Webster launches its online dictionary. It is now one of the most-used online dictionaries in the world.

Amsterdam, Netherlands, 2018 - The Institute for the Dutch Language maintains one of the largest dictionaries in the world. It has 40 volumes and is now available online.

2 Chapter Two

Tips for Using a Printed Dictionary

First, let's learn to use a dictionary that is a book. This is known as a printed dictionary.

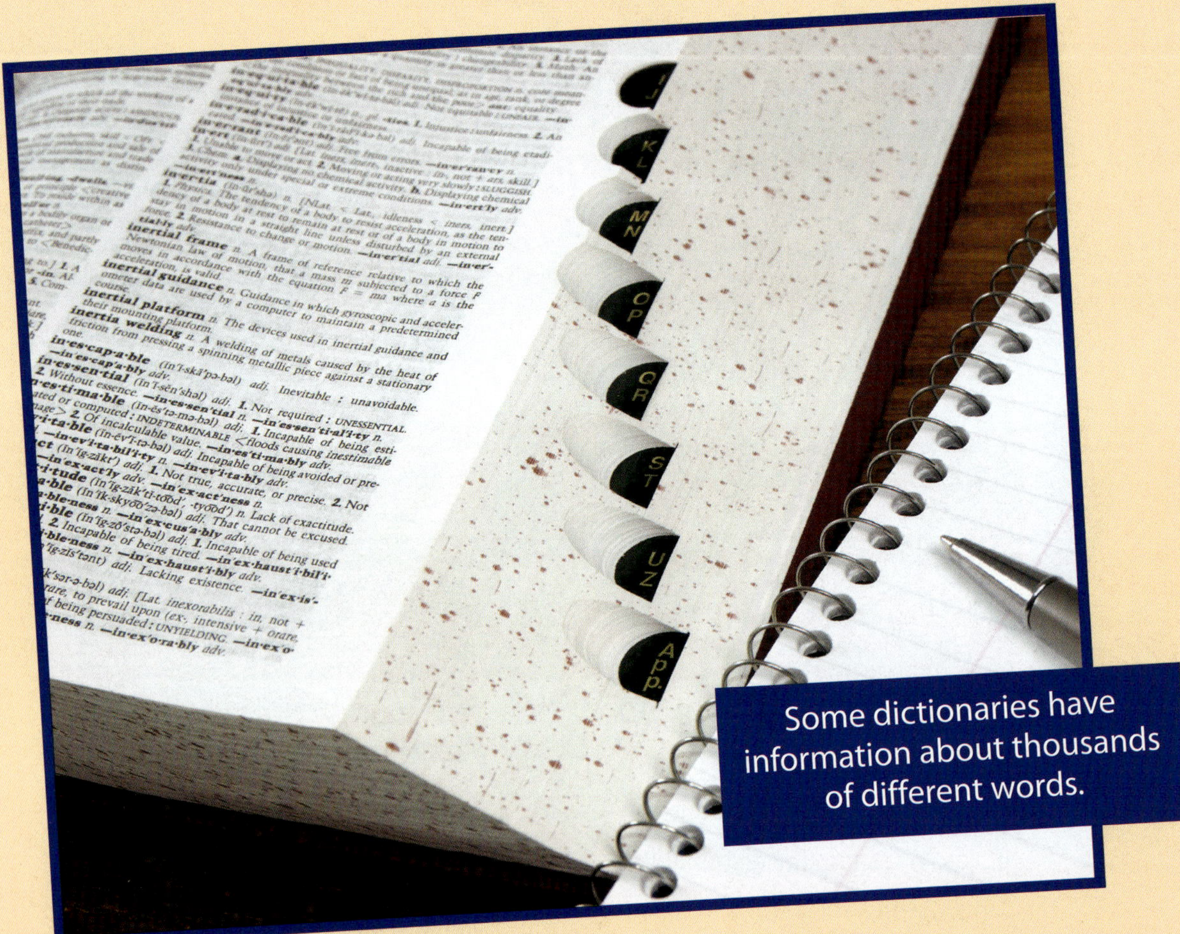

Some dictionaries have information about thousands of different words.

You need to understand **alphabetical order** to use a printed dictionary. The words are listed starting with the "A" words. Then come the "B" words. The words continue in order and end with the "Z" words.

A B C D E F G H I J K L M N O P Q R S T U V W X Y Z

In a dictionary, which word comes first, "octopus" or "queen"? If you are unsure, look at the alphabet above.

All of the words are in alphabetical order again within each letter section! Words are spelled using letters in a special order. Look at the order of the letters in each word. For example, look at the B section of the dictionary. "Baboon" comes before "baby." That's because of the alphabetical order of each letter in each word.

The first three letters of "baboon" and "baby" are the same. Look at the fourth letter to decide which word is first in a dictionary.

Printed dictionaries have **guide words** at the top of each page. These help you find your word. Guide words tell you the first word and the last word on that page. For example, one page might show all the words between "ace" and "ape." Ask yourself these questions: Does my word come before the first guide word? Does it come after the second guide word?

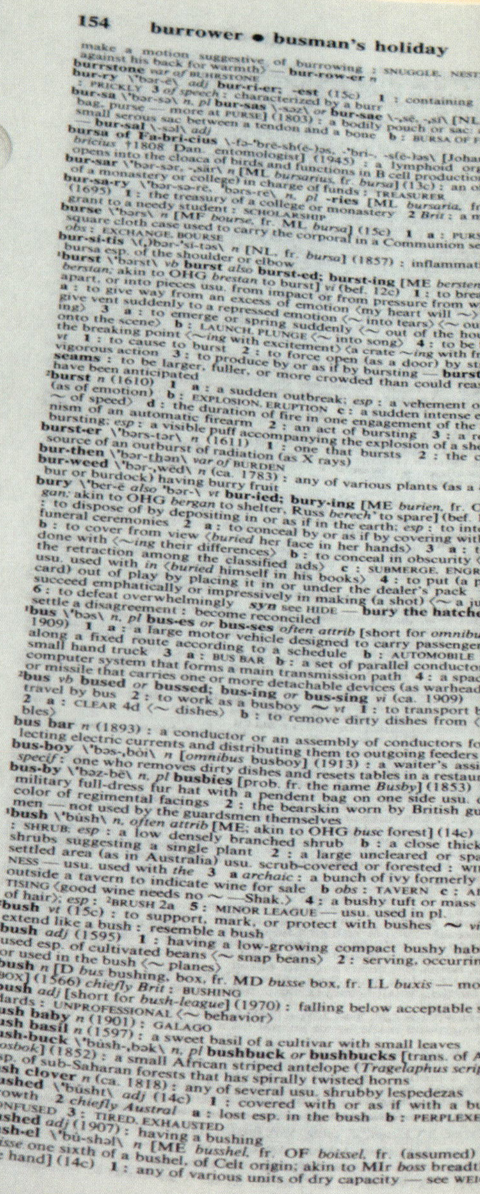

Use the guide words to quickly find what you're looking for.

Try This

You must know alphabetical order to use a printed dictionary. Let's practice! First, see if you can arrange the following words in alphabetical order:

bear   bed   banjo   bead   bake

Now let's practice using guide words. Pretend you are looking in a printed dictionary for the word "berry." The guide words at the top of the page you turn to are "bear" and "bed." Will your word be on this page? Will it be on the page before this one? Will it be on a page after this one?

Answer: bake, banjo, bead, bear, bed

You are correct if you said that it would be on a page after this page. "Bed" is the second guide word. "Berry" comes after "bed" in alphabetical order. So "berry" will not be on this page. It will be on a page after this one. You will have to turn the page and check out the next set of guide words. Keep looking until you find which guide words are a match. Then you can scan the page until you see your word!

3 Chapter Three

Get On with Your Online Search!

Now let's learn how to use an online dictionary. Many online dictionaries let you search for your word just by typing it in. But what if you do not know how to spell the word? Take your best guess. The online dictionary will take you to the word's **entry** if you spell it right. If you do not spell it right, that's okay. The dictionary will probably give you a list of words that are close to what you typed in. Choose the correct spelling. The dictionary will take you to the word you were looking for.

Do your best to spell your words the correct way.

Try This

There are many dictionaries on the internet. A children's dictionary is a good choice for students. You can find one by using a **search engine** page. A search engine is a computer program that helps you find information you are looking for. Some good search engines for kids are:

www.kidzsearch.com/boolify
https://www.safesearchkids.com
http://kidsclick.org

Many search engines even search dictionaries for you! Type in the word "define" and then type your word after it into a search engine. Can you find an online dictionary that is meant just for kids? Does your library website have any links to online dictionaries?

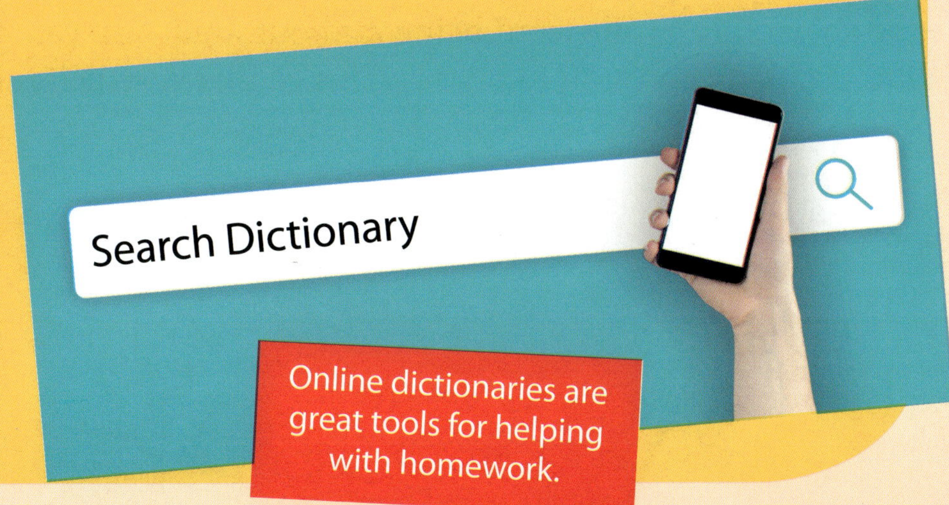

Online dictionaries are great tools for helping with homework.

4 Chapter Four

Unlocking the Secrets of a Dictionary Entry

An entry looks the same in online and printed dictionaries. Let's learn how to read a dictionary entry.

Let's look up the word "dog." In the entry, the word "dog" is listed in bolder or bigger letters. This lets you know that you are looking at the correct entry. Do you see the next bolder or larger word below yours? That is the start of an entry for a different word.

This entry includes a section that shows you how to pronounce the word. It might say that "dog" is pronounced "dawg." You might be able to hear your word being said out loud. You can sometimes click on a button to hear it. This can be very helpful!

Each entry tells you the **definition** of your word, or what the word means. There can be many definitions for each word. The dictionary points out the **part of speech** for each definition. The part of speech tells you what kind of word it is and how it is used in a sentence. For example, the word "dog" is both a noun and a verb! As a noun, it means the animal. The verb "dog" means to follow someone very closely. A dictionary helps you understand the different meanings.

“dishes”

“dish”

A dictionary also shows the spellings of words used in different ways. Sometimes you want to make a word **plural**. That means you have more than one of that item. The plural of “dog” is “dogs.” You add an “s” to the end of the word. Now you are talking about more than one dog. Not all plural words add “s” to the end. Some plural words add “es” to the end. One dish, two dishes. A dictionary tells you the right way to do this for each word.

There are **eight** different parts of speech.

Most dictionaries also include other words that are related to the entry. These words may help you better understand a word. The dictionary may also put the word in a sentence. That way, you can see how it is used. Some dictionaries even include pictures.

The **longest** word in an English dictionary, the name of a lung disease, is **45** letters long.

Try This

Find a printed or online dictionary. Look up the following words. What do they mean? Do they have more than one meaning? Do the definitions show different parts of speech?

	part of speech	definition
address		
lean		
stand		
run		
eye		
coat		
iron		
bow		
trunk		

Do you notice that many words have more than one meaning? The dictionary is filled with words that you may not know! You will learn something every time you use the dictionary.

What words will you learn next?

Quiz

1
Can a dictionary be a book, online website, or both?

2
What does a dictionary tell you about a word?

3
What did the Egyptians use to make a type of paper?

4
Dictionaries put words in what kind of order?

5
When did Noah Webster publish the first American English dictionary?

6
When did Merriam-Webster launch its online dictionary?

7
Can there be more than one definition for a word?

8
What do guide words tell you?

9
Do you have to spell a word correctly when using an online dictionary?

10
How many parts of speech are there?

Answers: **1.** Both **2.** What it means, the correct spelling, and how to pronounce it **3.** The papyrus plant **4.** Alphabetical **5.** 1806 **6.** 1996 **7.** Yes **8.** The first word and the last word on a page **9.** No **10.** Eight

Key Words

alphabetical order: an A-to-Z order, or listing things in the order of the alphabet

definition: an explanation of the meaning of a word

dictionary: a resource that lists words in alphabetical order and explains what they mean, how to pronounce them, and what part of speech they are

entry: a word that is listed in a dictionary

guide words: words that are found at the top of each page in a printed dictionary, which show the first and last words on that page

part of speech: the form of a word, such as noun, verb, adjective, or adverb

plural: the form of a word used for two or more of something

pronounce: to say words out loud

resource: something you can go to for help, such as a dictionary or encyclopedia

search engine: a computer program that helps you find words or information you request

Index

LIGHTBOX

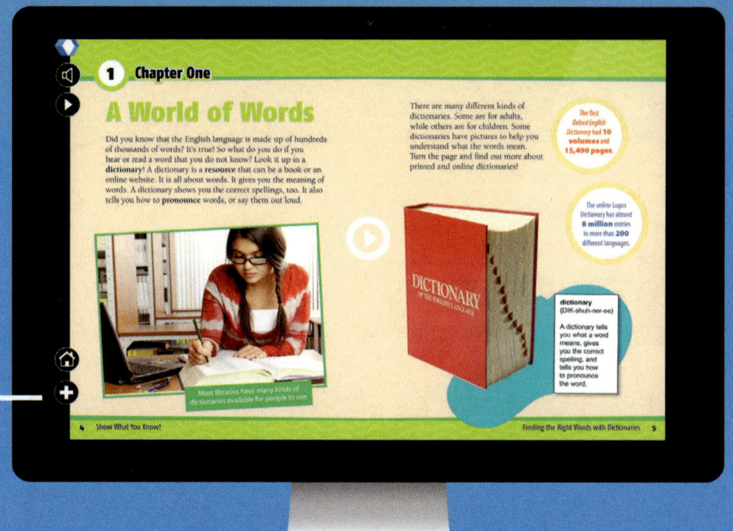

SUPPLEMENTARY RESOURCES

Click on the plus icon ⊕ found in the bottom left corner of each spread to open additional teacher resources.

- Download and print the book's quizzes and activities
- Access curriculum correlations
- Explore additional web applications that enhance the Lightbox experience

LIGHTBOX DIGITAL TITLES
Packed full of integrated media

VIDEOS

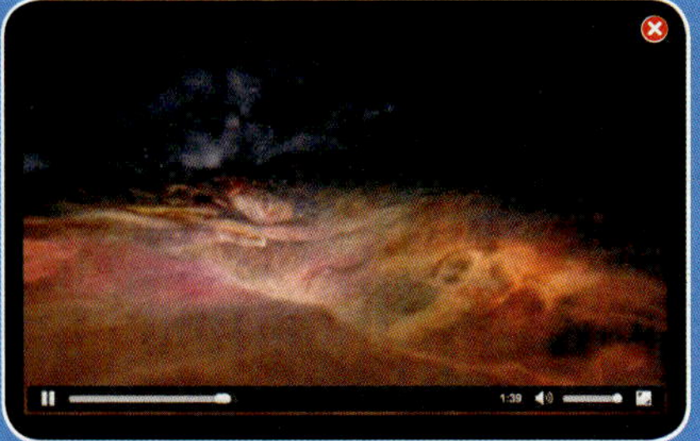

INTERACTIVE MAPS

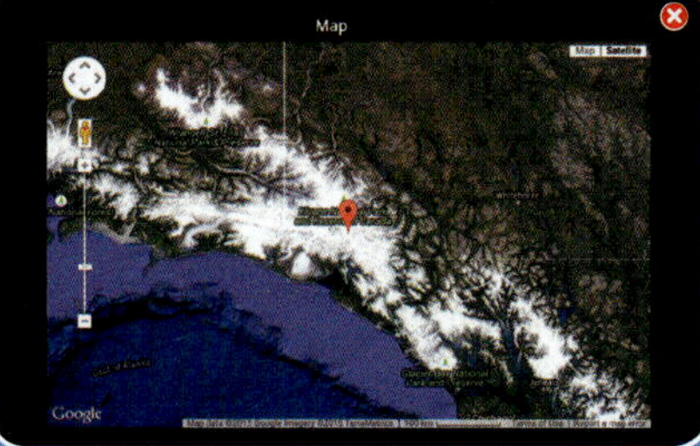

WEBLINKS

SLIDESHOWS

QUIZZES

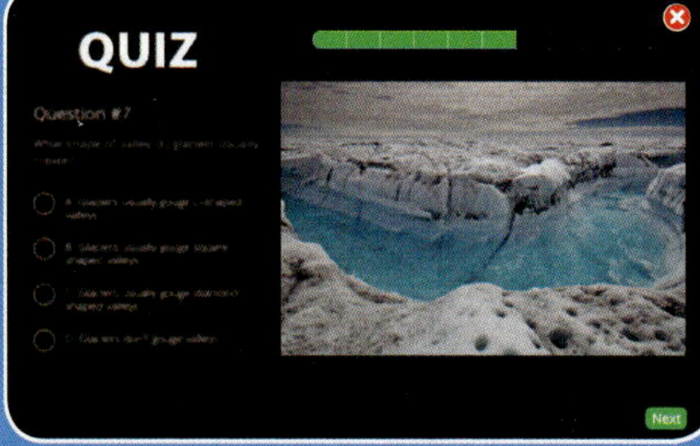

OPTIMIZED FOR

- ✓ TABLETS
- ✓ WHITEBOARDS
- ✓ COMPUTERS
- ✓ AND MUCH MORE!

Published by Smartbook Media Inc. 350 5th Avenue, 59th Floor New York, NY 10118
Website: www.openlightbox.com

First published by Cherry Lake Publishing in 2013

Library of Congress Control Number: 2018941476

ISBN 978-1-5105-3979-2 (hardcover)
ISBN 978-1-5105-3980-8 (multi-user eBook)

Printed in Brainerd, Minnesota, United States
1 2 3 4 5 6 7 8 9 0 22 21 20 19 18

062018
120517

Project Coordinator Heather Kissock
Designer Nick Newton

Photo Credits
Every reasonable effort has been made to trace ownership and to obtain permission to reprint copyright material. The publisher would be pleased to have any errors or omissions brought to its attention so that they may be corrected in subsequent printings.

The publisher acknowledges Getty Images, Shutterstock, Alamy, and iStock as its primary image suppliers for this title.